A Season of Birds

Dion Henderson

illustrations by Chuck Ripper

Tamarack Press

Madison

Also by Dion Henderson

The Waltons: The Bird Dog
The Wolf of Thunder Mountain
On the Mountain
Hunting
The Last One
Algonquin

598.2
Henderson

Library of Congress Cataloging in Publication Data
Henderson, Dion, 1921-
    A season of birds.
    1. Birds—Addresses, essays, lectures. I. Ripper, Charles L. II. Title.
QL676.H48   598.2   76-21044
ISBN 0-915024-07-1

Designer: William T. Pope

Printed by Litho Productions, Inc.

First Edition

For Beth, who shared the two worlds,
within and without

WINTER

I am continually dismayed by those people who think that they are, in and of themselves, independent of the wild community. We are all in this together.

Ernest Swift

WINTER / INTRODUCTION

The woods are gray, a steely wind cuts across the crusted snow, and fair-weather friends long since have flown. Here, on the acre that is home, a winter day brings a fresh interpretation of brotherhood.

The band of comrades in my yard this day can be colored motley, in spirit as in feather. It is made up of chickadees and juncos (which have almost no enemies), starlings and sparrows (which have almost no friends), a vainglorious blue jay, and waxwings and cardinals and a visiting redpoll. The earthbound are part of the group, too: a desultory skunk, a fretful mouse, and across a dusting of snow, the mysterious hand-and-foot prints of a possum, bisected by the telltale imprint of a careless tail. And then, of course, there are the squirrels at practice on the arching flights required to reach the bird feeders, and rabbits in the comic mold of Sir John Falstaff.

Thus here we are together, a random crew, impressed to serve an environmental outpost within the wide hedges, where the red pines and the spruce shoulder up through the multiflora thickets, and the milkweed pods stand starkly above the snow. In summer we may go our separate ways like a scattering of cousins, with one another's lives as far from thought as sight. But now we are drawn close and share the common purpose: to stay merry when we may, and warm when possible, and fed if we are able; but above all, to stay alive until there is spring again.

There will be hard days, and some wild ones will not endure. Some will be eaten so that others may eat, and some will simply die, a surplus wiped away. Deep beneath the surface of this basic fact, a worm of wonder stirs and turns: how did we come together here, and why? Why, for instance, does a bird stay here when it could as well have flown another thousand miles south? Why does the insect gourmet remain cheerily in this place where most insects sleep, so that it must live by substitute and alternative until the warm nights bring fresh stirrings in the larval burrows?

And why are we here, and why do we stay?

At night the moon makes sharp black shadows on the snow. Some of the shadows move and leave tracks like rabbits' and others, more like an owl's wings, leave none. Always there are more questions than there are answers.

9

WINTER / CHICKADEE

In winter the ax bites sharply into a tree, and toward it hastens the chickadee. The ax on the kindling in the woodshed has no such effect, with its thuds and ragged sounds of splinters. But in the woods, if there is the crack of wood struck and the steely tone of the ax, presently there is black-capped company come to dine.

Dining, it is well to remember, is the serious business that brought the company, with bib tidily in place. Chickadees learn early that the sound of an ax on a tree may mean a treasure of ants disclosed in the hollow of a rotten oak, or a locust tree riddled by borer and full now of all sorts of frosty tidbits for the probing beak.

I can forgive this forthright greediness more easily than many another gaucherie by a friend, because it is based soundly on necessity and carried off with grace. If the luck is all bad, and the fallen tree is only a box elder with scarcely a hibernating spider to be found, the chickadee will do a day's duty as gay company anyhow, as though it did not matter.

But of course it does.

The chickadee will eat insects if he can, and seeds if he can't, and crumbs if there are neither; and if all fails, he dies, rather easily. Despite the fact that the little black-capped fellow is a creature of our winters, he is not ideally equipped to stand the strain. His heating system must burn more brightly and use more fuel than the other winter birds. To live, a chickadee must stay fed, and dry as well, and out of the wind.

That is why he comes so quickly to join me in the bright, wintry woods, and will follow me all day in the sun, but will not follow me across the open space where the wind may get behind him. And that is why a chickadee will not come to a feeder that faces the wind; he dare not. It is why he must have heavy cover against the damp cold, and be clear of January thaws, and have a hollow birch or shaggy hickory to hide in. This bright and cheerful bit of fluff has few enemies in the wild, except the wind that comes from the northwest by night and searches out foolish little birds that strayed too far by day.

At this time of year the chickadee makes the call that gives him his name, which he is willing to exchange with his listener at length, in tones ranging from the solemn to pure banter. He has a song or two as well, but saves them for their season: the spring whistle of two notes, and another of three that I think is more often heard in the fall.

In the summer the chickadee is easy to overlook. But in the winter, when a fellow needs a friend and is close to woods where the snow is brilliant in the sun, and a dead tree stands stark against the blue-and-white sky, he need only lift the ax and sound the dinner bell.

WINTER / MOUSE

The bird feeder in the cedars had gone a month unattended and might have gone longer except for the cat that sat beneath it, emitting plaintive yowls of frustration when no bird was in sight.

A lifting of the roof and a peek inside the hopper told the story: A portly mouse was there ensconced in grain, with all such temporal threats as cats walled away. It glared crossly at the interruption and left only when pulled out firmly by the tail.

Obviously this mouse, being not only imaginative but lean and hungry with the foraging of winter, had found the feeder, slipped through the narrow opening where the grain drops into the trays, and settled down to a life of ease. He had eaten until he was too fat to leave as he had entered; hence he had to stay until all the grain was gone, and he had hungered and grown thin enough again to get away.

Lean and hungry we came into this world; lean and hungry do we depart. The fat time is the middle time.

For a house mouse the middle time is comparatively short. He has a potential longevity of six years, though he averages only two. He has ways of compensating for his life's brevity. A young mouse may take up family duties of his own at the age of eight weeks, and there may be a new litter in a month. In recent years the mouse population has been relatively stable, although in most places it is more than enough to provide a mouse for every man, woman, and child.

It is likely that the house mouse arrived with the other colonists at Virginia and at Plymouth, although it wasn't until 1852 that Increase Lapham reported it present in Milwaukee. This is the great mouse of all the world, the cosmopolite, who can be found on every floor of a city skyscraper. This is the mouse whose color mutations give some small boys pets with which to frighten some small girls chosen for the special favor; whose psychic mutations provide the dancing mice; whose white body is the ideal laboratory for biological, genetic, and medical research. And with all this, the mouse still may sing, sounding something like a cricket but generally at a frequency inaudible to human ears.

If the house mouse has few really efficient enemies, he also has few friends, although he is friendly enough and easily tamed. It may be that, except to those miscreant boys and a Scots poet here and there, he has too many of mankind's own tastes to be trusted. In any case, it all may be in the point of view. What is enterprise to the mouse is burglary to my bird feeder, and the felon is exiled to the woodpile, thus reducing the profits of crime and terminating a chapter of the fat middle time of life. Now the cat sits no more beneath the feeder, and the siskins are back.

WINTER / WAXWING

Yesterday the cedar waxwings came to call.

At a time of year when the world outside the window is so deficient in notable events that the congregating of three rabbits beneath the bird feeder is recorded faithfully, the coming of the waxwings ranks with what Pooh called Very Significant Occasions.

It isn't the sort of thing that the geese will do to you a month from now, you understand, when an old gander leading his long gray line back toward Horicon Marsh will sound his trumpet in the murky spring night above your uneasy pillow, and you will sleep no more.

No indeed. The cedar waxwings, as a matter of fact, haven't been anywhere. I have seen a pair here, a family group there, from time to time all winter. But now they are banded together—cousins and relatives and perhaps a few good friends. Suddenly they came past the window, a fragmented arrowhead of birds wheeling together and landing, fifty or more in motion together, lining up on the branches of a mountain ash that was planted beyond the den window for this very purpose. They came, and stayed a day—big cheerful, elegant birds, decently subdued in voice, and splendidly mannered.

Six of them sat on a foot of branch. The bird on the end plucked a berry and passed it on to the bird at the other end before it was eaten. This is a courtesy exhibited by no other songbird in our land, and which would be denied by naturalists if it were not so readily observed wherever waxwings gather. Not that they are entirely saintly: A passing of the berry was seen outside the window where the fifth bird in line fumbled, and the crest on the last bird rose in indignation. Then the clumsy one was given a good whack for dropping the tidbit.

After a few minutes' observations, individual birds are recognizable, since there is considerable variation in their garments. There are a dozen shades of fawn and gray and olive, with the black mask universal, and various options on the yellow trim marking the tail, and on the bright red waxlike appendages on the wing secondaries. Ornithologists use the term "imperfect plumage" for birds without the bright yellow band or the beading, but it seems an impolite reference.

At any rate, they came calling, and will come again, for the sulky young witching tree still is heavy with berries. I hope they will look over the elms as well, for while waxwings do not deal heavily in insects, they make a specialty of elm bark beetles and thus are twice welcome.

When the bright berries are gone, the waxwings will move on, and we will be left with such Insignificant Occasions as the three rabbits waiting hopefully for the juncos to scratch unwanted sunflower seeds out of the front feeder. At least until the geese come.

WINTER / RABBIT

An apple tree is for more than the making of apples. It is for a catbird nest, and a wren house, for the soft snow of blossoms, and the storm of warblers, for climbing in and falling out of, and, finally, for a fragrance on the hearth. Yet great purposes may be served inconspicuously: I might as well admit that I prune my apple trees in February, so that the rabbits may make love with full stomachs. The question is not whether man, whatever his intention, should contribute to the prosperity of rabbits, but how. I do not know what rabbits did hereabouts before I came, bringing the apple trees, but I think it is certain there were fewer rabbits.

Not that rabbits are so single-minded and relentlessly specific in their foraging. They will, if winter brings the necessity, eat anything in the way of shrub or sapling; at the peak years of their ten- or eleven-year cycles, they will eat virtually everything. The annual rings on any oak stump provide a reasonably valid index to the years of rabbit scarcity, since oaks rarely sally forth successfully into top growth except during the low of the rabbit cycles.

In the Midwest we have a modest assortment of hares, but for all practical purposes only one rabbit, known in books as Mearns' Cottontail, who was here waiting when the first settlers came, and who, presumably, rejoiced. Although there is no record of the northern range at that time, the rabbit moved north with the plow and the hoe, and especially with the planters of apple trees; in 1907, the old writers tell us, the first rabbit was recorded at the far end of Lake Superior. It may be that with the coming of the exurbs the rabbit attained his finest hour. Acre lots are admirably set out for a sprinter who can travel at some eighteen miles an hour but not for much more than a hundred yards. All of rabbitdom can appreciate tidy husbandmen who brook neither weasel nor fox, ferret nor skunk, who have driven off the owl and the hawk, and entertain only complacent pussycats and nearsighted dogs in the way of predators. In the wild a rabbit may require as much as forty acres of woodland edge, but in the suburbs he may run two to the acre, and three or four times a year considerably more.

It is here that the rabbit stands before man and his philosophies in the splendor of biological contradiction: Short of stamina, low on vitality, easily affrighted, and seldom enduring beyond two of his potential eight or nine years, the rabbit flourishes. A man who would take one out of his garden and expect to reduce the resident population might better try to diminish a well with a teacup. The levels of wells, and of rabbits, are determined in other quarters, and on other grounds.

17

WINTER / OWL

W hile most creatures desperately wait out the icy siege of today, the great horned owls busy themselves with the business of tomorrow. From the crude platform nest of a departed crow, deep in the woods, a head amazingly like a cat's is raised. The owl must huddle unremittingly over its two white eggs in this weather, when the life within could freeze in minutes.

The eggs might have been laid as early as the end of January, and there may even be three of them. But they were put into the nest several days apart, and will hatch that way, with one owlet older than the next. Ornithologists have speculated that this staggered hatch reflects complicated planning, but it seems a simple arrangement to spread out the demand when the food supply is low. Because they incubate when the year is most inhospitable, horned owls must feed their fledglings with prey not yet past the low of its annual cycle, when it is least nutritious. But this too may be an integral part of an ecological system within which a wild community evolves the limiting factors and biological controls that suspend its members in bearable ratios with one another. For the great horned owl is one of nature's supreme predators, and wild communities can support only so many of them, as long as there is limited room for rabbits and mice. So the owl, for reasons it does not know, brings forth its young when survival is most difficult. A fledgling owl may eat rabbits—the food of choice in the wild—along with songbird and game bird, unwary squirrel and strayed poultry: whatever is available that will stoke the fierce furnace of life. The great horned owl is one of the few hunters that prey upon the skunk, being either immune to the potent defense or heedless of it, and a little later in the season it will take woodchucks, gophers, and even insects.

The big owl has an enemy to fear, as do the bear and wolf, and for the same reason: His interests frequently conflict with man's, and the owl, like the others, must always be the loser in the end. When an owl finds a chicken yard, for instance, he is likely to lose perspective. It is recorded that one owl took fifty-nine young turkeys from a ranch in one season. There is no cure for such a taste but death.

Still, the woods at night is a different place when there is no unearthly voice to ask the four-syllable question that occurs to owls. Without him, who indeed?

19

WINTER / PURPLE FINCH

Winter brings a quartet of playboys to the bird feeder among the spruce. They look like sparrows who late on New Year's Eve fell headlong into the wine. Their sober brown suits are discernible enough through the claret stain, but heads and vests are as richly colored as the bursting grape.

These are the purple finches, gone a-gypsying in February, when they are most appreciated. In May, when the fruit buds are swelling, they are welcomed with some misgiving, although the number of buds they eat is a small price for their transient presence. But now they wade into the seed in the roofed feeder, demonstrating notable prowess. One makes a specialty of sunflower seeds, a formidable item to a picker of ragweed, but in a minute by the watch he splits and gobbles five with his thick, dark beak.

Called purple grosbeaks by some, although little more than half the size of their chisel-headed cousins, purple finches in summer are generally found far from orchards. They prefer the pine barrens and the conifer marshes in nesting season, which means that while a man's fruit trees generally escape their attention, he also misses their spectacular courting flights and their songs of spring.

They have little to say now, in the feeder, or in the trees nearby, or even scurrying about in the snow for wayward seeds. Somehow, though, they are more vivid than they seem in summer—almost a gaudy red against the white snow, where even such steady eyes as Fuertes and Gromme saw them tinted pink. Perhaps they really are brighter at this season. Perhaps they only seem so, as full winter brings a weariness for things drab and dull, and an appreciative eye for wine-stained finches.

21

WINTER / SISKIN

More things change than the landscape as my conifers come of age. Where once the bare branches of native shrubs knew only snowbird and jay, chickadee and sparrow and cardinal, now strangers swarm among the greenery. Goldfinches in winter dress seem another bird from the bright summer visitor; the redpolls burst into an open space like thrown handsful of feathers; and suddenly there are pine siskins.

All of these birds, and more, are attracted by the evergreens, by the cones and seeds of cedar, spruce, and pine. In my small manipulated environment, ecological succession proceeds solemnly in miniature, following the vegetative pace of a few hundred trees.

It is better, however, not to count on the siskins longer than you can see them. They are the jet-setters of their society; what is in today may be out tomorrow, and this year's passion may soon be forgotten. There have been landlords who entertained great flocks one season and then never saw the bright brown birds again. And, presumably, there may be some who play host repeatedly and assume they shelter some kind of sparrow. Siskins do not have the flaring kind of costumery that demands attention. They are handsomely patterned in a quiet way, with brown streaks and white trim, but it is in sudden flight that they disclose the canary-yellow tinting in wing and tail feathers.

There is more to the kinship, of course, than color, and these are all finches—siskins and redpolls and the wild canaries. Although each has his own special music, they share enough basic melodies to make the ear an unreliable agent in telling which is which, and when. Once the snow is gone, all will feed enthusiastically on maple and elm, and afterward on ragweed, although the siskin will maintain his preference for the dark green forest.

The constancy is in the inconstancy. The siskin is no bird for lovers to swear by, but it is a philosophical reminder: What is here in nature may not remain forever, whether transient birds or the verdure of the earth.

23

SPRING

Saturday, April 20. Art Hawkins and I spent the day at the Leopold shack on the Wisconsin River near Baraboo. High points—a pair of mallards feeding in the front yard marsh, a big hen woodcock flushing from an inky black pothole, grouse droppings three inches deep under a grape tangle, two deer bounding across the road, a pet squirrel and Mrs. Leopold's stew.

The Journal of Clay Schoenfeld

SPRING / ENGLISH SPARROW

26

Some must await the first sight of a robin to predict confidently the imminence of spring. But it has been a long winter and I have accepted the announcement of a common sparrow. She scratched away the remnant of snow in a flower bed to bare the mulching hay, selected a long stalk, and flew upward toward the martin house to begin a nest. Winter has worn out its welcome with the sparrow hen and me. We are both sick of it.

It would be strange if now, some hundred years after this cockney gamine first settled in Brooklyn eight pairs strong, that at last it has found useful employment even though of no more consequence than a vernal forecast. An aggressive and physically advantaged exotic, the sparrow was set down in an environment where evolution did not have centuries to make the necessary provisions to balance it with other species. The stranger flourished then, as now, at the expense of native birds and to the detriment of its habitat, to say nothing of its social standing.

But what nature would control, it must first make dependent. Thus the sparrow of the city street and village lot depended at first upon the horse. The horse is gone, victim of an accelerating age, and the population of sparrows has dropped well back into the reduced carrying capacity of its range. The city streets have starlings now, but sparrows are too practical to throng forlornly in the wake of beer trucks.

The sparrow has few enemies, but a century of civilization has had its effect on the onetime guttersnipe. He still is bold and cocky, loving a fight for the fight's own sake, and he keeps his small home area in a condition most charitably described as alert. He still takes his toll of unwatched eggs—but so does the wren. And if there is not an old birdhouse on the premises, he still will build in the garage and roost without fail over newly washed automobiles or just above the back door.

But a sparrow has his good points, and not the least of them is his attitude toward his late-arriving cousin, the starling. As the patron saint of burglars said, it takes one to know one, and the sparrow has no doubts about the character deficiencies of the starling. If the starling builds a nest, the sparrow will tear it apart, and if the starling leaves eggs, the sparrow will account for them. After several such experiences, many a frustrated starling will pack up and leave, while the sparrow stays to stand guard over the neighborhood.

My sparrow hen is making another trip from the flower bed to the martin house with a wisp of hay, and I salute her impatience. A perceptive prophet needs only a modest signal to proclaim the season, if he's ready. And I am.

SPRING / CARDINAL

The resident cardinal has taken up his household duties again, bringing confirmation to the prior uncertain signals that spring soon will be at the gate. The bedraggled robin, after all, may have only ridden a balmy thermal current one day too long, and the blind crocus bulb fooled by the reflective basement wall. But when I open the back door there occurs what may be described by a word familiar in the social dialogue of our times: a confrontation. This bird with whom I have dwelt in peace—nay, friendship—upon this acre all winter, sits insolently in the butternut tree a rod from the door, demanding an explanation of my presence, and questioning the validity of my title. He has taken over the property.

However, the indignation of the vermilion crest moderates with grudging recognition; after all, we have counseled together these past months upon the need for fresh supplies of sunflower seeds, and upon redressing offenses attributable to visiting pussycats, and he may concede that there is room upon the grounds for my family as well as his—if we are careful.

This greatest of the sparrows has all the style and character of the landed gentry. It is no wonder that half the southern states where plantation aristocracy flourished tried to claim him by appending their names to his.

Like our other sparrows, of course, he is a finch, but he has nine feathers in the hand section of his wing, and twelve in the tail, though that is not what matters. What matters is the shrill two-syllable whistle echoing from the treetops—the sound a young male makes when he sees an unattached female in the spring, or wishes he did, and the lower flute notes with a final cheeky chuckle. Imitate him, and you may have an affair of honor on your hands: He will respond instantly, and keep it up, and track you down, until he is in the tree nearest you, bristling with pride as he checks his domain.

And what matters is the way he sings to his mate, whiling away the time when she is brooding or when she leaves the nest to bathe and groom, and how he takes over management of the first batch of young birds while she sits up on the second clutch of eggs.

But what matters most is simply his presence, particularly in the dread time of winter when the light is close to death. At the nadir of the year he shows the scarlet flash of promise that all this will pass, and that it is best endured with a dash of elegance and grace. And when his whistle comes in spring, you know he was right.

29

SPRING / CROW

In the midst of a great city, a cry filtering through a mile of leaden sky turns the heart suddenly homeward, and memory toward spring. Harsh and clear it comes again, then between the buildings sweeps a line of crows, a fierce squadron of aerial pirates beating strongly through the sooty air toward a refuge in some city park.

When I was young they came that way, in a ragged skirmish line over the fields, then across the lake and up the hills to roost among the prickly Virginia cedars, where they were safe from owls.

There are no owls here to disturb the sleeping knavery of crows, but certainly nothing so simple as safety would bring them to the city. More likely they have laid a course, and part of the city lies below, and they care nothing about it one way or another. If a thing is not good to eat, or worth acquiring—and if it does not shoot—then a crow will ignore it. Eating and the acquisition of material things, especially those belonging to others, are habits responsible for much of the crow's conflict with mankind. In a day when there were more crows and little boys did not have so much to do, many nestlings were abducted, at some considerable peril to the little boys, and brought up as pets. And yes, some talked, after a fashion, with or without the barbaric splitting of tongues.

All such crows were universal thieves. In the wild they were detested by farmers because of their taste for newly planted corn: not hard, dry corn, you understand, but planted and germinating, with tender sprouts and the dry starches all turned to sugars in the cells. A flock of crows could sweep away a young cornfield in an afternoon. A scarecrow might give protection, but only for a day unless it held a gun, and even then, some hunters swore, an experienced crow not only could tell that it was a gun, but its gauge and range as well.

There is no question that crows are nest-robbing predators, but they are not very efficient at it. The pursuit of songbirds is hard work for a big, unwieldy bird. A crow's food pattern leans far more heavily to insects—June bugs are the food of choice in nesting season, and some young crows are stuffed almost exclusively with them. Crows also eat toads and frogs and crawfish and other dainties as they become available. Since the automobile became a major predator on small game populations, the crow has taken on another useful purpose—cleaning the roads of carrion.

Some people claim to have heard crows warble melodiously when secluded; it may be so, but it could not be more welcome than their springtime racket. The raucous shouts of homeward-bound crows sailing down into the sunset is a sound of spring as welcome in the city as ever among the cedars on the ridge, when I was young.

SPRING / RAIN

Sometimes in spring there comes a rain with special properties. Before it, the vernal growth stands poised, swollen and waiting; after it, all things thrive.

There are annual signals that summon the scene changes of the world of nature—now bringing on a riotous flood of life, now setting it silently to ebb. Some of the calls are as imperceptible as the footcandles of light intensity, which change each day with no effect, and then suddenly send the great geese up into a thousand-mile procession. But the rains of spring are simpler and more predictable in their effect. There have been showers before, where the earth soaked up the moisture sullenly and waited; these cold, searching rains of spring leave the green world dissatisfied and sulking.

Then comes a night when there is a feeling of sultry heat, and when the rain begins, the steam rises. The rain is warm, and smites you with the great rank, fertile, green smell, as the darkness stirs and breathes.

Life's cycle turns for its beginnings to the same components with which it started a million years ago. This rain, for what reason no one can say with certainty, is the right rain—the required additional moisture, or perhaps the essential degree of temperature. The algae among the lichens awake, the buried spores stir, blind mouths hunger in the soil. In the morning the maples will flaunt their tiny naked flowers, and the water in the ditches may bear thin cloudy strands of frogs' eggs. Seeds that lay dead in the ground today will turn. There will be a green haze of weeds in the garden, and a robin looking for a worm.

SPRING / WREN AND ROBIN

Those who think that man's woes are peculiarly his own, that the sweet simplicity of our furred and feathered colleagues avoids such things as ethnic strife and civil disorder, could be enlightened by a walk around my garage.

At the rear there is a wren house below the eaves, a splendid screen of young spruce a few feet away, and the gardens spreading out in view, teeming with the endless potential of beetles, worms, caterpillars, spiders, and other fauna among the flora. Among the several wren families on the premises each year, this choice location belongs to the wren that can scold the loudest, longest, and with least repetition.

This year there were complications. The new roof on the wren house brought on the trouble: The old one had been sharply pitched, but the new one followed the contemporary trend of being flat, and hinged at the back to simplify the annual housecleaning.

In April the flat roof, tucked cozily beneath the garage eaves, attracted a pair of honeymooning robins. They knew nothing about the box beneath the roof, since they couldn't get their heads into it anyway. But they could sit on the shelf and look out on the garden, and speculate pleasantly on the summer bug cycle, and dwell on the happy coincidence of cherry trees and plums and highbush cranberries and such. Hence the robin nest rose magically on the flat roof of the wren house, and two eggs were deposited, and the robins were sitting smugly on them when the wrens arrived.

It is possible that wrens and robins have spent too much time as intimates of man. Each pair was certain of its own just cause, and righteousness sounded clearly in the complaints. The wrens considered themselves sat upon by squatters, their domestic privacy invaded, and their tranquillity outraged. They took up stations in the spruce and began to deliver a series of stirring addresses on the subject of robins. After a few days the robins looked a little frayed but they held firm, and the wrens indignantly decided to move into the lower flat anyway.

The wren houses around our place are perchless, and require a certain speed and agility of those who pass back and forth. The wrens soon found that if they paused at the opening, they could expect a severe peck from the brooding robin above. They eliminated this peril by not pausing as they popped in. The wrens drew a fine sight from thirty feet away, and once zeroed in, whizzed through the tiny door. The robins became very nervous, sitting on their nest as howitzer shells passed underneath at uneasy intervals.

But soon the new baby robins were able to fly, and the parents thankfully moved away. Down at the other end of the garden, now, a couple of haggard-looking robins are living in a scrub box elder tree. There are many better places for a nest in the nearby hedges, but these robins don't seem to be interested. So much for strife and disorder.

SPRING / ORIOLE

A friend tells of an oriole that was seen salvaging threads from a trellis; the bird was offered short lengths of bright yarn, and the swinging basket in a nearby elm began to develop in the hue and pattern of a Norwegian sweater. Then the surplus yarn ran out, and the bribed bird, corruption shamelessly plain in its behavior, landed on the screen of the back door to complain. When there still was no more yarn, the oriole left in a huff, abandoning not only the screen, but the yard as well, and its fashionable nest.

This might be a pretty fable from which one could infer that whoever trifles with the affection of a wild creature should be prepared to bear the emotional scars of disillusionment. But the potential venality of orioles, as of the rest of us, is well known and varies only according to the availability of attractive bait.

The incident brings up an old controversy which has led a number of ornithologists to heated discussions and cool relations ever after. One school, for instance, which included the redoubtable Mabel Osgood Wright, maintained that the oriole would never use any strange material of other than somber hue. Mrs. Wright reported an incident almost identical to ours, but in her account only a single bright scarlet thread was woven into the nest; then the bird's character reasserted itself and the nest was abandoned. This, Mrs. Wright believed, was because of the red thread, or possibly because of a red squirrel living in the same tree, an observation that tends to weaken the whole point.

On the other hand, John Burroughs told of spending two days watching an oriole homemaker happily weaving his offerings of crimson, orange, green, yellow, and blue yarn into the nest. He noted, though, that the bird used the yarn only on the top of the complicated structure and stuck to hemp and grasses in the lower portion, for the sake of ventilation.

At any rate, there is some evidence that the oriole, which has perfected the nest-building technique pioneered by the vireos and some warblers, has achieved an advanced stage of adaptability in use of house-building materials. That is the important thing from a biological point of view, for from such simple observations grim theories are promulgated. A creature that makes the necessary environmental adjustments by using what is at hand is numbered among the mice and rabbits, the starlings and the human beings of the world—creatures that adapt and will not become rare before their time.

SPRING / THRASHER

An overpowering overture swept through the yard the other morning. Children tumbled out of bed, windows popped open, and the puppy took a valiant stand at the door, prepared to fall in her tracks if necessary. The tide of sound was coming from a telephone pole in the corner of the garden, where a bird not much larger than a robin was turning up his amplifier so loud that it seemed as though his feathers might be blown off.

There was no doubt about it. Big Daddy was back.

Some people mark the turning of the season by the calendar, but full spring does not come to my premises until its clarion is sounded by the returning brown thrasher. Not only is spring's clarion sounded then, but also its piccolo, trombone, string section, and percussion, interpolated by musical whistles, an imitation of a calliope, and a few bars taken from the book of the original Memphis Jug Band.

Those who know the thrasher count on a relationship of continuing surprises; individual birds apparently add to their repertoires as long as they live. Of the three great mimic thrushes, the thrasher always is placed ahead of the catbird as a musicologist, and usually ranked behind the southern mockingbird. That evaluation does not necessarily hold on a bird-for-bird basis. In fact, the thrasher is called the brown mockingbird over much of the range he shares with the southern mocker. And like that good gray bird, the thrasher has an accurate ear for whatever sound may attract its attention.

Unlike the catbird, which generally plays it straight, both the thrasher and the mocker are splendid improvisors, able to integrate a collection of widely varied noises into an original composition of superior quality. When a catbird is fascinated by the sound of a squeaky bicycle, he repeats the sound of a squeaky bicycle. When a thrasher or a mockingbird picks up the racket, it is transformed into an impression of a squeaky bicycle as composed by Berlioz and performed by the London Symphony Orchestra. Year before last, for example, Big Daddy put together a popular number that combined the song of a visiting warbler band, Number Two Daughter's high school flute solo, and the delightful noises made by the milkman carrying a rack of empty bottles.

Our Big Daddy does more than sing. His corner of the garden is his alone, from the top of the pole to the somewhat careless nest constructed in the sprawling rose hedge. He terrorizes pussycats, he has starlings ducking hastily into the martin house, and for the next six weeks our backyard baseball games will be played with third base moved twenty prudent feet away from the nest. Big Daddy has already defeated three baseballs and a fielder's glove in hand-to-hand combat.

Such adjustments are the price paid for playing host to genius. Maestro has his foibles, his eccentricities, but the rites of spring would not sound the same under any less boisterous conductor.

SPRING / WARBLER

Now, in fulfillment of what Emerson called "the trusty almanac of the birds' first coming back," when the apple blossoms are heavy on the bough and the plum trees spread their scent across the lawn, come the warblers.

They come in a stunning hail of color and song that flicks out, touches, and disappears. There remains the bewildered and mildly dissatisfied feeling of one who has had a splendidly ornamented dream, but who cannot remember exactly what happened.

Partly this is due to the confusion of numbers. On this continent there are some one hundred fifty species of warblers belonging to twenty-one genera; there are a dozen different kinds in my yard this afternoon, and there will be another dozen, entirely different, tomorrow morning. I turn my head and a tree comes alive with a host in motley; I turn again and the bright throng is gone. If one is not content simply to witness, but must confirm specifically what was seen, a color chart might help thread the way through the maze of individual identification. Striped with black and white, were they? Then they were one of four that are colored so. Black and red? Surely, that one, a redstart. But olive above and yellow below? Then it is one of fifteen species, and lots of luck in picking out the details that make the difference.

But specific identification does not really matter, except to those who must make lists and gloat upon them. The coming of the warblers is a thing to be experienced. It is a thing to be prepared for and to be witnessed, lest because of its quick arrival and departure it is missed altogether, except for the vague impression of a dazzling moment.

The blossom-eaters, warblers are called, but they are not. Because nearly all of them are wholly insectivorous, they come with the blossoms and can be seen there, peering into buds, plucking at leaves, whisking from twig to twig for the bugs that are awakened to a new cycle by the same photothermal processes that awaken the tree.

The individual habits of these diversely dressed travelers range from the arboreal, who spend virtually their whole lives aloft, to the terrestrial, who seem to be afraid of heights.

It is unlikely that any one among us would become expert of warblers from his own observations alone; there is too much, in too little time. Some of the birds, of course, stay with us and we sometimes forget that they are truly warblers and give them pet names—the chat, the ovenbird, the yellowthroat. But with most there is a blur, and perhaps an eerie echo, and a sense of something having passed us without recognition.

This is a small thing, but if there is a tragedy in wastes, here is the heart of one: to behold without really being witness, to be party but not participant, to know but not to understand, to let an irretrievable moment of life slip by, heedlessly unaccounted.

SUMMER

Like other great landowners, I have tenants. They are negligent about rents but very punctilious about tenures.

Aldo Leopold

SUMMER / BLUE GROSBEAK

44

If you were seeking evidence to support Thomas Wolfe's lament about "wandering forever and the earth again," you would not think to look toward the pool in my backyard where the water reflects the white fan of birches bending over it. But there was a flash of darkly iridescent blue there the other afternoon that brought to mind what Wolfe found in wandering—"a dark miracle that brings new magic in a dusty world."

There was the flash of blue, and a little boy whispered excitedly, "bluebird." He is a connoisseur; only one bluebird has been seen here in his seven years, and he was the one to see it. But this was not a bluebird, no old familiar friend coming back after the long, lost years. This was a blue grosbeak, so rare in the north that there are hardly a dozen significant records, so retiring in his southern woodland home that the authorities grow somewhat waspish when discussing whether his song does or does not resemble the purple finch's.

There will be no asperity here, and no clarification. We only *saw* him, a slender lance of glistening blue darkening in the long tail, the rufous chevrons on the wing, and the unmistakable profile of his clan. He paused, drank, and was gone.

But he was there.

I think that Audubon did not paint the blue grosbeak from life, although if the bird were common anywhere it would have been within the span from Louisville to New Orleans, where Audubon himself wandered. Wilson did not paint him at all; Fuertes and Gromme rendered him dutifully; and there is a color photograph by Thase Daniel that you know has life truly in it once you have seen the living bird. But this is ornithology, which is poor stuff if taken straight. It is good enough, for instance, to know that this bird feeds its young a varied menu of insects and, when they are grown, goes back to a diet of grain.

Speculation begins when you wonder why. There is no exploding population pressure to force the blue grosbeak northward here, as the bobwhite quail came once and stayed, or for that matter, that forced the whitetail deer southward into the streets of Chicago. There is no environmental factor working, not one that would bring the wayfarer to be recorded only a dozen times in a hundred years. There may be explanation enough in a spark of impulse, and a hill that has another side to see, and across the valley a lush new field, and then another hill, and as Wolfe said, of wandering forever and the earth again.

The nature faddists would have man believe that he left no kin behind him in the sea, and brought no heritage with him from the trees. But life is life. In my mind I travel a little way with this small creature who, out of a million birds that lived and died content at home, had to see the far side of the hill.

SUMMER / DOVE

Shortly after the first robins are firmly in residence, the first pair of mourning doves comes whistling through the trees, heedlessly intent upon their chase. Tennyson linked the doves and young men's fancy as two irrefutable signs of the season, but in truth these two notable signs could be taken jointly as the signal for nearly any season. As far north as Ohio mourning doves have been found nesting in every month but December and January. Incubation takes only about two weeks, and in our climate extends from May until September. It is easy to find fresh eggs in a nest still occupied by previous fledglings who are too young to fly.

As others have learned, the practice of love rarely makes one perfect in more mundane activities. The nest of the mourning dove, to bestow a certain dignity on it, is an example. A robin makes four better nests than this while getting ready to make the ultimate model. It is not so much that dove eggs are likely to fall out of the nest as it is they are likely to fall through it. And if the parent nods at her task, she may fall through as well.

There was a time when the dove took the happier choice of the alternative decree—to migrate, or to stay and outnumber the opposition. Now it tries to do both. Those that winter in their northern homes are safe among the songbirds, but those that travel south become game birds cherished by southern hunters. You may never see them, the old men used to say, but you'll hear the whistle of their wings.

Whatever her shortcomings as a housekeeper, the mourning dove makes up for them as a mother. Like all pigeons, she is maternal beyond all reason and may be seen sitting protectively on a couple of young louts who are so large that she must sit on them crosswise, with their heads sticking out from under one of her wings, and their tails from under the other.

The dove's flight is unmistakable, the sweep and sibilance of it; the male alone is responsible for the spring aerial acrobatics in which he rises nearly straight up, with much noisy wing-flapping, and then comes as sharply down, perhaps to the same perch.

The person who took the dove's call for a funeral chant and described it as "mourning" must have been a doleful fellow, too much alone. It is a coo, as in "bill and coo," and the worst thing that may be said of it is that on some occasions it sounds tired.

SUMMER / FULLNESS

48

N ow the time of bounty has come upon the land. Scarlet globes bear down the cherry trees, purple clusters drop from their wild cousins, and in the thickets black raspberries glisten among the briars. On the burdened boughs blackbird and robin, blue jay and catbird, kinglet and oriole sit, if not in peace at least in silence, their mouths stuffed too full to quarrel.

It seems only a few days since the jay was skulking in the shrubs, waiting for the sparrow to leave its nest. While the sparrow was absent on its own dastardly mission of raiding the wren, the blue assassin darted in and flew away with a half-feathered sparrow child. While this was going on, the neighborhood tomcat wreaked murder on the jay's own carelessly built nest, and thus perpetuated predation's chain, the predator of one moment the prey of the next.

But now the time of largess has come, the burgeoning, lavish fruiting of the earth itself, the beginning of the harvest that will pour on like a torrent until the frost, and afterward. The product of the flowers of spring hangs heavy on the branch today, and flowers budding now will hold seed pods fat above the snow.

The survivors of spring's bloody business flourish, robin and rabbit, bat and butterfly alike. The cottontails sit carelessly in the clover, too stuffed to stir until the dog's questing nose sniffs coldly in their inattentive ears. In the cherry tree a grackle not only declines to fly away, but raises a hoarse question of basic ownership on one branch as the householder climbs along another.

It does not matter. There is enough to feed the insatiable youth of a hundred families native to this acre—not only the half-grown rabbit and the miniature squirrels, but the young jays in their bright new suits, and the robins in spotted weskits, and the olive oriole youngsters. The gorge of summer lies ahead, and gluttony is the order of the day.

SUMMER / HUMMINGBIRD

A hummingbird comes to the hanging feeder a few scant inches from the breakfast table and hovers in cubic flight: up and down, back and forth, in three dimensions. In the early light he is bronze and green and purple and velvety black, with a great vermilion throat patch that suddenly is definitely gold instead, then possibly even green, as his angle to the sun changes.

The spectrophotometer expert tells us this is because his colors are structural rather than pigmentary; it is easier to understand that as a kaleidoscope depends on movement for its shifting patterns, you see the splendid color changes best in the living, restless bird. An iridescent bee, Pearson called him. A Pilgrim father writing home to England from Plymouth Colony reported, "Ye Humbird, no bigger nor a hornet, a wonder of the countrey." And Audubon described him as "a glittering fragment of the rainbow."

He is more a wonder than the unicorn. Where a crow flaps his wings three times a second in normal flight, a rubythroat may go as high as two hundred, changing the pitch of wings in the process so that a stroke in any direction is a working stroke. A one-hundred-seventy-pound man using the equivalent in energy would burn up one hundred fifty-five thousand calories a day, and evaporate one hundred pounds of water an hour; without water, the temperature of such a man's skin would rise above the melting point of lead.

The operation of the three-inch furnace boggles the fancy; if the hummingbird did not exist, engineers could prove he was impossible. He must refuel fifty or sixty times a day—every ten or fifteen minutes of daylight. Because he cannot feed in the dark, each night he enters a state roughly similar to the great annual hibernation phase of mammals: The functions slow, the temperature drops, the hot torch of life burns perceptibly lower, so that there will be embers left at morning. But this same flittering mite flies five hundred miles across the Gulf of Mexico to winter in Yucatan. No one knows how he feeds during this passage. He does not fly more than thirty miles an hour even in spurts, but he survives some twenty hours or more of transoceanic flight.

Shops are full of glass balls with drinking tubes designed for easy access by the rubythroat's divided tongue, a tongue that rolls up neatly to make two drinking straws for lifting nectar from deep within a flower. Filled with red sugar water to attract the small bright eye, such a feeder will have instant and repeated attention in hummingbird country. Yet perhaps it is too easy; those who record such things have noticed that frequently hummingbird populations decline in areas where the red sugar water is too accessible.

There is a temptation to draw a moral, but it will be resisted. Let the sugar water be fortified, and appropriate flowers kept in bloom along the hedge, and the proliferation of small spiders encouraged for the rubythroat to supplement its dextrose diet. Giving up the feeder just beyond the window is giving up too much, too soon.

51

SUMMER / TOWHEE

The report that a white-breasted robin was frequenting our premises turned out to be erroneous. The eight-year old eyewitness who led us forth and pointed it out in triumph thereby learned something about the untrustworthy standard of always believing what one sees. The visitor was a common towhee, scratching busily beneath the dogwood like a Rhode Island Red hen in pursuit of supper.

But better-trained eyes have made worse mistakes, and older judgments have compounded them. The towhee also is a finch, and shares the familiar cheeky attitude. Called ground robin, or marsh robin, among other things, it is not rare among us, but since it is a bird of the deep forests and the big bogs, it is seen infrequently by patio ornithologists.

The towhee has been the subject of heated discussions among field biologists. All of them know well, for instance, that no bird has the vocal equipment to pronounce true consonants. Still, there are listeners who maintain that a towhee's call can be written "chewink," followed by what sounds like a trilled note—except that all musicians and some biologists know that a trill is alternation between two notes of differing pitch, instead of a single tone. There are a number of ventriloquists among the songbirds, and the towhee is one of the best, although the catbird may have a better act. The towhee can sing from three or four different places, and never reveal his exact location.

Since he nests traditionally well away from man, the towhee has no great reputation either as a friend or enemy. If he came to the garden in robin numbers, he would be received with the same mixed emotions. He is a destroyer of insects, bane to bugs but also to predaceous beetles, seed-eater—yes; and he also consumes cherries, grapes, and berries. The location of a towhee's nest explains the alternate name of ground robin, although you might have to trail a local cowbird to find one. By some quirk, cowbirds dote on towhee nests, hidden though they are. Despite the fact that towhee eggs and nestlings are bigger than the cowbird's, as many as six cowbird eggs may be laid in a towhee nest before the host loses patience and either ousts the lot or moves.

We may have a chance to observe it all firsthand, because another eyewitness has testified unwittingly that we have a pair of towhees with us now. My son accounted for a female with a brownish coat, and a neighbor down the road reported that she saw a white-breasted "oriole" the other day. The conclusion, my dear Watson, is obvious.

SUMMER / BLUE JAY

An uproar develops in the pine beyond the window. Branches thrash, there is a flirt of gray tail, and a patch of blue emerges, shrieking of a theft most bold. They are squirrel and blue jay, jousting for the acorns piled in an old robin's nest—likely by neither—and using strong language toward one another. What each one says is true; it takes a thief to know one.

By and large, I do not hold with those who translate the sounds birds make into English words: This bird says thus, and that one so. A musician can score the songs of thrushes and play them on a flute, but there is no way to spell the laughter of a loon, or fit words to an eagle's scream. And yet, a blue jay—especially a blue jay caught in aggravated robbery—yells, "Thief!" and there's no more to be said about it.

Theft, it might be noted, is one of his more attractive activities. This vainglorious knave is one of the continent's most beautiful birds and one of what the righteous would call most wicked, except that moral terms are not really applicable to natural behavior patterns. Possibly I'm partial to rogues in general, but it should be noted that we are deplorably lacking, birdwise and otherwise, in villains of the first order—villains with taste and style and high humor to match the depths of their skulduggery. The blue jay qualifies on all counts. His sense of comedy has attracted raconteurs since the time of Mark Twain. He is a dandy, musician, ventriloquist, and mimic. He is also called a nest-robber, with justification, and cannibal, without. In truth, more than three-quarters of the blue jay's annual diet consists of vegetable matter. Boring and scaling insects and their eggs, noxious beetles, and grasshoppers form nearly twenty percent of his diet. Predaceous beetles contribute nearly four percent, which is a mark against him, and one percent remains for mice, fish, and snails—as well as other birds, or eggs, which he certainly takes in season.

So it is with all things wild, and some not so wild. If you want robins, then you must give up a few cherries; if you want a blue jay, give up a robin's egg here and there. In turn, the owl someday will make the equation complete.

SUMMER / STARLING

The lessons taught by poverty are largely bitter lessons and better left unlearned. This is a concept as true in the wild community as in any other. A man preserves a functional sanity through long years of prison by feeding a sparrow. Good for him and for the sparrow. But if he tells you that the relationship achieved with the sparrow made the walled-up years worthwhile, then it would be better if you think him mad.

There are hints of the season around us. The mockingbird is gone from the lawn, where soon the frost will glisten at morning; the thrasher does not greet the sun with orchestral virtuosity from the yard's highest tree; the shadows haunted by the catbird since the end of May are very still. But a friend who sifts morbidly through the summer's waste and loss says, "Well, the mimic thrushes may be gone, but at least we still have the starlings."

We do, indeed. The observation has the same intuitive wisdom as, for instance, telling a man who has just fallen out of a bee tree that while he has no honey, at least he has not been stung. If he has not broken a leg as well, he may kick you for thanks.

The fact that the starling is a mimic, if a poor one, is little known or heeded by those who would rather dislike him for his basic character. If you insist that a good thing be said of him, let it be that occasionally he eats bugs, although the knowledgeable gardener, given the choice, would rather have an honest bug any time. This short-tailed blackbird is a housebreaker, home-wrecker, despoiler of eggs and fledglings, a grotesque harlequin in ugly living color whose awkward mimes signal despoliation of nearly every yard and garden bird we favor, from wren to warbler, thrush, robin, and martin to flicker. The starling is powerful for a bird its size, possessing a bone structure which provides extraordinary leverage, a bill that is long, heavy, and sharp, and a skull almost as strong as a woodpecker's.

It is said that the first successful importation of starlings from Europe came with the release of eighty birds at New York's Central Park in 1890 by Eugene Scheifflin. Since the only other exotics that can be mentioned in the same breath are the Norway rat and the elm bark beetle, it is not recorded what grudge Mr. Scheifflin had against his native land to inspire the importation. Within eighteen years starlings had spread through New York, much of New Jersey, and into Pennsylvania and Delaware: The plague was irreversible.

If ecology has said anything to its poor disciples, it is the whispered word that a time may come when, given the choice between the starling and nothing, it might be better to choose nothing. The bitter lesson is, however, that such a choice is rare, and no matter what manner of mess we have made, we must live in it, and live it out. But there is no need, for virtue's sake, to find merit in the lesson.

AUTUMN

When is a weed not a weed? What should you cut and let grow? The law says thistles must die, but now that they are ripe the wild canaries sit like golden birds on their nodding white heads. Who is to say whether the wand of wheat that the thistle kills is more important in the scheme of things than the bird the thistle feeds?

Mel Ellis

AUTUMN / NIGHTHAWK

Summer is like love; it may wane and then grow strong again, but at the final going it does not diminish gracefully and imperceptibly and finally, like a whisper, fade away. It simply stops. There is an end to it.

So it is that a golden morning comes, the sun is warm, the grass is green beyond the window, and the roses push up their tall, splendid, third-stage blooms, but when you open the door there is silence. The wrens are gone and summer's dead. By twilight there will be a sudden noiseless swooping in the open places and you know that it is time to turn to other things. The nighthawks have returned and autumn is all about you, brought on softly-beating, white-barred wings.

Prophet follows prophet; the white-banded wing of the nighthawk cleaves the twilight like cold wind cutting through the warm night. Thus nature hangs a lamp of warning in the window. The baleful message bears too heavily on such a small bird, concerned only with gathering the family on insect-heavy evenings to feed for the flight south. Like the martin, swift, and swallow, the nighthawk must follow the buzz of airborne insects. It is, indeed, no hawk, nor does it resemble one. Instead of taloned feet, it has toes almost too weak for perching, and instead of the fierce beak, it has a wide-spreading, bristled mouth, the trap of the mosquito hunter.

It is in some justice called a mosquito hawk, but it is called other things with less reason, like will-o'-the-wisp, for instance, which the whippoorwill is called as well. But the nighthawk is also called goatsucker—a self-explanatory and clearly preposterous name, however firm in folklore. And bullbat is a term still used in some places, although how it came to be a colloquialism in a time when both bull and bat were better known is hard to understand.

Whatever else it is, the nighthawk is unmistakable in flight: the graceful bent wing, the fluttering climb, and the breathless dives. Surely the name "hawk" comes from the way the bird reaches the top of its aerial ladder, pauses an instant, and then pitches over the lip of an invisible precipice in a breathless swoop—like a falcon stooping to the kill. It seems a spectacular flight for so small a prize as a fly or beetle, and it brings the nighthawk close to the disaster of a treetop, or even of the ground. But it is part of the performance, as recognizable as the innocent spectre itself, with the telltale band of white across the sixth, seventh, eighth, and sometimes the ninth primaries of its long, pointed wings, and with the male additionally marked by a white band across his tail.

So they come, heedless of the dread message they write against our sky, intent on carrying out their responsibilities. We miss the wrens and see the nighthawks with a stirring of uneasiness, and even resentment, because they bear bad tidings. Was it thus for those who carried the grim words to Sparta from Thermopylae?

AUTUMN / GRASSHOPPER

A lime green grasshopper comes from nowhere and plunks onto a lily pad in the pool, falls off, swims strongly to a rock, climbs up, and is gobbled eagerly by a bright-eyed robin waiting impatiently among the flagstones. For robin and blackbird, for grackle, jay and catbird, for hawk and sparrow alike, this is grasshopper time, when the champagne breakfast begins at dawn and lasts until dark.

Among the yard and garden birds that are insectivorous, as well as among those that will accept an insect only when the cherries or raspberries or plums are not handy, grasshoppers in season must be listed as the unquestioned food of choice. The birds are like small children left alone in a chocolate ice-cream factory; they eat as though there were no tomorrow, or at least no food for it. I suppose that in good grasshopper areas, many fat, feathered diners subsist entirely on grasshoppers during this time. A bird may eat so many within this period that grasshoppers may form ten percent of his annual diet.

The pièce de résistance under discussion here eats as well as he is eaten. He belongs to the vast order that includes biblical locusts and Mormon crickets and other orthoptera of historical stature. One kind or another of his tribe can be a major pest to fruit, forage, grain, and anything else green and tasty.

He is, in turn, not only a banquet for birds, but for skunks, shrews, mice, moles, and toads too. Various wasps sting him to paralysis and stock their nests with him to feed their young. And most of the creatures that eat the adult grasshopper will eat the eggs and nymphs, as the latter pass through their six or eight stages, gradually looking more and more like grasshoppers in what is called an incomplete metamorphosis.

Yet the grasshopper flourishes, spits tobacco juice fearlessly in the eye of the foe and on the fingers of little boys, and draws the bow of his long hind leg across the violin of a forewing in his autumnal mating song. Spring is not the only time for wild romance. The adult stage of a grasshopper's existence is reached in time to deposit eggs where they can endure the winter safely and begin the cycle anew next year.

Our katydid is one of the longhorned grasshoppers, called so for the segment antennae nearly as long as the insect itself. He is no migrant, and seldom as great a poet as his cousins—a musician rather than a menace. He also has long been cited as a bad example, when compared with the ant for thrift and industry.

But not by me. My delegation casts its vote unhesitatingly for the grasshopper, who dares to light the lamp of love and sing against the threat of coming death, who scorns the monstrous mechanistic order and safety of the anthill.

AUTUMN / OVENBIRD

In the growing debris of leaf and bract beneath the walnut, the butternut, and the birch in the microcosmic forest beyond the pool, an ovenbird strolls casually, but in high style. The sport coat is fashionably cut and smartly olive, and if the contrasting weskit is a bit plump, the fault is familiar, and one that the hard winter's work will remedy. But this fellow only plays at dignity. The pontifical pose is intermittent, and suddenly put aside. The tail bobs preposterously, and suddenly this substantial member of the warbler clan is scuffling in the duff for a fat fall worm. Wagtail, they called him once, although to a fellow brought up among four-footed tail-waggers the vertical motion of the ovenbird's caboose is bobbing, not wagging.

Common in our climate, and welcome, the ovenbird is confused with other thrushes by many who miss his abundant personal credentials. There is this business with the tail for instance, and then he walks. Most terrestrial birds either hop or run. Only the ovenbird, the crow, the starling, the grackle, and a few others can really walk. And the ovenbird has a blond streak on his head that tells you plainly why Thoreau knew him as the golden-crowned thrush and so named him more than a dozen times in his journal, even if he did not know his songs.

There are two songs, but only one is clear and common. My younger son, perhaps sensitized to things academic, contends the bird says, "TEACH-er," or sometimes "teach-ER." He did not learn such things from me, this twisting of birdsong into the likeness of human speech, but he has good company in it: John Burroughs thought the bird said the same thing, and stridently. But it is the flight song that is the mystery. At twilight in early summer, the ovenbird mounts from branch to branch in ascending fury, voicing a song as lyrical as any thrush. He emerges like a small skyrocket in a burst of color and song at the treetop, only to fold his wings and dive like a lark toward the dark ground again. This flight is what Thoreau never was able to detect, and fretted about.

Perhaps the melodic arpeggio is like the ovenbird's proud and hearty stride, belonging to an image we may find inconsistent. How easily we become presumptuous in our interpretations. There's nothing inconsistent about the bird's behavior; inconsistency is in the eye of the beholder. And yet I wonder. If Shelley had seen and heard the portly stroller instead of the lyric aerial grace of the skylark, would he have been inspired to write solemnly, "To An Ovenbird"?

AUTUMN / SPIDER

In the eerie, strained light of an Indian summer afternoon, the southward-tending sun glints on gossamer strands floating against the cobalt sky. Birds are not alone in being born to fly; there is an older, easier way: lighter than air. And the young spiders are setting sail late this year.

Not that any kind of courageous choice is involved. The young spiders were perhaps a late litter, dwelling together in the maternal web until their internal yolk sacs were absorbed, a signal that their digestive systems were mature and they were at last able to eat. With the awakening of hunger came the awakening of fear, or at least the instinctive drive to escape, and the little ones scattered. They had to, for those which did not scatter would be eaten instead.

Each spiderling, climbing a piece of grass, or stone, or even clod of earth, aims his spinneret at the sky and puts forth a filament into the wind, and perhaps another, until his wonderful balloon of tiny strands pulls him free of earth and carries him away. This aerial dispersion of young spiders is shared by many species. Aircraft have found the tiny sailors five miles high, and they have drifted among the masts of ships a hundred miles at sea.

Even if they come down in a favorable environment, the tiny travelers must scurry about while they go through as many as thirteen moults before they become adults, able to deal with living prey. Not all spiders spin webs for insect snares—although all spiders have the remarkable equipment in tubes and spigots on their abdomens—but all share a dietary limitation: None can ingest solid food. Hence, a bug taken in the web must be immobilized by silk and then bitten. Poison is injected by the spider's fang, and digestive enzymes are injected afterward, to carry out what might be called exterior digestion. Only when the inside of the captive is liquid can the spider sup, and when he is through only the familiar chitinous shell of the beetle or wasp is left behind.

Spider silk is finer and lighter and stronger than that produced by a silkworm, but the threads in a web are not single strands. The silk is extruded as a liquid, which turns immediately into the solid filament, and the filaments are woven into a cable by the arachnid engineer. The abdominal spinneret is one way you may know a spider from any other creature, as you may know him by his two body segments and four pairs of walking legs.

But in the long, gold twilight of the waning season, the phenomenon is not so much the capacity to produce silk as it is the demand of nature that it be put to use, and the young which could as well pass the winter in the egg are flung out upon the vagrant charity of the air.

AUTUMN / GEESE

n the backyard, a small boy and a dog are suddenly immobilized at their game, and their eyes turn upward, seeking the source of distant clamor in the cold gray sky.

The geese come into sight, a great spearpoint cleaving the high firmament of an autumn afternoon. Boy and dog are rapt until the fleet has gone its way, beating remorselessly along the thousand-mile trade route of the armadas that follow summer home from the mouth of the MacKenzie and Melville Island and the great tundras beyond the trees. Then these two of mine go separate ways, bemused, their game forgotten after passage of the geese.

There are a dozen species on the continent, but when we speak of geese we speak of Canadas. At the way stations like Seney and Horicon and Orchard Lake that stretch south from the arctic circle, there may be a mingling of Richardson's and White-Fronts, and more Snows if they came from the western provinces, or Blues if they came from Hudson's Bay, but they are dwarfed both in size and numbers.

The Canada geese of old October are not like the gamblers of spring. In March they come—singly, or in constant couples, or in scattered bands—their talk loud and importunate. In the distance they sound like the yelping of nervous puppies as they discuss the wager of a long night's flight in windy dark against finding a break in winter, betting cold and hunger and the risk of other hungers against the occurrence of a patch of open water or a forgotten corn shock. Geese, after all, are not committed to the water; they are better designed than ducks, with the landing gear moved forward so they can walk as fast and as easily as a man, and they will nest if they must in an old hawk's nest on a prairie mound.

But now in autumn the tall gray ships go sailing by, distant and aloof, in sixes and multiples of six that speak of family groups, with the authoritarian two-toned honk of patriarchal commands cutting through the youthful gabble of the season's young, tightening the lines of childish stragglers in the rear.

I do not know what it is in the clangorous speech of distant geese that speaks directly to the soul, or even what it says, but there is no denying the deep stirrings of response. Certainly we do not yearn after geese solely because of their freedom, or their disregard of earthly possessions, any more than we admire them for the nobility which is no more theirs to mold than it is ours. I do not know what the passage of the geese means, only that it is a signal that was, and may still be, of vital import. I cannot speak for the dog in the backyard, but I can speak for the boy, having been one: He has communicated with another country, and his thoughts are far from home.

AUTUMN / FLICKER

A long the woodland roadside a covey rises. The birds are big as partridge, but partridge they are not. Brighter than the bright leaves of autumn in which they were scuffling, with whites and browns and velvet blacks to go with the scarlet neckpiece and the flashing gold of wing and tail, it is a flicker family, convened for a final fall reunion. If there were any doubt, it would be dispelled by the flight, which has been described as an aerial gallop, and the whickering cry. Documentation is inconclusive, but this group appears to be a mated pair and the year's young, apparently from several nestings because there are a dozen birds together. Many are immature, wearing their father's handsome black mustache which the young ladies of the tribe will discard at maturity.

Those who have lived close to flickers have a special feeling for this big, cheerful, gregarious woodpecker, and I have lived in such propinquity as neither I nor the flicker family really intended. There was a hollow red cedar six feet from the cabin door, and a pair of yellowhammers set up housekeeping while the cabin was uninhabited. Their main entrance was head high, facing the cabin door. Every time I came out of the building and let the screen slam, one or two, or later six, would burst out of the cedar with a yodel, and if I happened to be carrying something, either I dropped it or threw it over my head. They were good neighbors, but they found a quieter place to live the next year.

Flickers are good neighbors for other birds as well. They will mingle with robin and sparrow alike, and are one of very few indeed who seem undismayed in the company of crows. If anything, they are likely to be victims of their couth: If a starling takes a fancy to a flicker nest, he may badger the big bird into leaving it. "Nest" is a charitable description of a flicker residence: It is an excavation, done industriously by the male, frequently while two or more females dispute who will be his bride. Whatever the decision, the bride will not be satisfied with the nest, but will chip away on the inside to make a small heap of wood fragments on which to lay her eggs.

Like most of the forty-odd kinds of North American woodpeckers, the flicker has four toes, evenly opposed, and a long cylindrical tongue, pointed and barbed and a splendid tool for withdrawing grubs and insects from infested trees. The tongue is a structural marvel, beginning with filaments of bone that curl up the inside of the skull. But a flicker's digging equipment is not the best in the tribe. His tongue is not quite so barbed and his beak is not quite the best of chisels, which is one reason he putters around the forest floor, rousing the fauna of the duff. Since his animal food is almost entirely harmful insects he is a welcome forester.

But he has another value more difficult to measure, unless you can put a value on how the heart lifts at the sight of him, and at his boisterous yell. When a flicker spreads his wings, he puts a flash of sunshine in a gray November day.

71

AUTUMN / SNOWBIRD

The snowbirds have come back, like a squall swirling and eddying around the backyard, and I suppose I should conclude that if the birds are here, then snow isn't far behind. That may be true enough, but of course the birds have nothing to do with it. What their coming means is that the days grow shorter on the western shore of Hudson's Bay, and the nights cold enough to inhibit the growth of fat bugs, and weed seeds are fine but there's a life of luxury just a few days away.

There is something endearing about a bird whose idea of retreating to a mild climate is to sally as far south, say, as Milwaukee. A man can be at home with, and even feel affection toward, a wild bird that dwells by choice where he himself dwells by necessity. It is well enough to announce the sighting of a mockingbird and log the passage of the warblers, but two months hence, when the year fades slackly close to death, there will be chill white mornings when we feel a kinship with the crow, and hesitate to broom the house sparrows out of the garage, and there will be active pleasure in spreading banquets of seed and suet on the feeders.

The snowbird is a slatey junco now; his nomenclature is subject to change, and probably will soon be changed again. I learned him by that name, although there was grumbling that I called him so. My children were taught both names for a selfish reason of my own: On Christmas, when the world is white, I want to hear they are watching snowbirds, not *Junco hyemalis*. The new name is no great gain, as most such titles are, to aid in identification of habit and family. It derives from the Latin for seed, and might as well be the name of any other sparrow.

What matters is that they came, with cheery wisps of conversation. Friendly but not tame, they swarmed over the dead flowers in the garden, finding special favorites among the compositae, playing like smartly tailored children on the last big leaves in the lily pool. A dozen discovered that they might light upon a leaf and it would sink—but only an inch or so, before the bulk displaced their weight. They splashed and splattered with dangerous zest until they were too wet to fly, and had to hop damply across intervening pads and climb a rock to dry.

Not all that came will stay, of course. But some will choose our acre, and be here in spring, and the dark months will be a little brighter because of them.

WINTER AGAIN

Orion stood due south at midnight
on the night that I was born.

WINTER / SHRIKE

A neighbor reported that he had never before seen a blue jay kill a sparrow at his bird feeder, then fly away with it to a locust tree, impale it on a thorn, and devour it. It would not have been tactful, or particularly instructive under the circumstances, to observe that he hadn't seen such a thing on this occasion either; people develop a remarkably prompt commitment to things they think they saw. It is rare at this season to see a shrike do such a thing, and that, of course, is what my neighbor saw. For a reason that eludes me, a man who sees and understands the industrial averages at a glance will look at a northern shrike and see a blue jay. Perhaps it is because he knows the blue jay and not the shrike, and one sees what one knows. It is true that shrikes come only irregularly among us now, a development gratifying to juncos and chickadees, to say nothing of sparrows.

This bird is of a blue jay's size, bluish-gray and white, with handsome black trim, but he is only a casual look-alike. It is his membership in the order of perching birds that has induced his telltale habit of impaling dead prey on a thorn, or splinter, or barbed wire, or handy nail. It is not a cache, as some would say, and certainly not cruelty, which is a characteristic largely confined to the ultimate primates. He does it because his feet are a songbird's feet, engineered for perching and not for rending food, as a hawk's are. His feet are not strong enough for him to sit and hold his prey and to tear pieces from it at the same time, without upsetting himself. Thus he spikes it on a handy thorn to give himself leverage.

It has been noted, with disapproving overtones, that shrikes kill and impale victims which they then carelessly leave uneaten, as though the fun were in the spilling of the blood. It may be so, but squirrels bury nuts and forget where, and in nature there is no more immorality in a wasted sparrow on a locust thorn than in an acorn wasted in a hollow log. This is part of the basic equation that supports nature's prodigality: There must be so many acorns to make possible a squirrel, and so many sparrows for a shrike. The surplus is not waste, but only insurance that the factory will not run short of raw materials needed for its more extravagant models.

WINTER / MISCHANCE

The saw's singing is interrupted by a piercing screech; the big raker teeth draw forth flickering sparks from the cut on the base of the tree. Never did the maple tribe grow with heart of stone, but stone it is that grates against the saw. When at last ax and wedges do their work to finish the cut and topple the tree, what stopped the saw is plain. There at the tawny heart of the trunk is a chunk of granite half the size of a man's fist.

There is no explanation, only speculation. This tree was one of a clump of suckers that grew around a now-vanished stump. Perhaps a boy threw the rock at a dodging rabbit, or it was pitched by a passing plow and lodged between the sapling and its parent. The tree must have grown around the stone, the stump cleared away, and the other saplings cut in turn until this one was left. By then the stone had been engulfed by the fibers. There is only some irregularity on the trunk outside to tell of the youth's injury.

Somehow we rarely stop to calculate the perils in the wild, perhaps being too much concerned with perils of our own. I had never before seen a stone within a tree. But there is fire and lightning, the heedless passerby twisting off the leader of a sprout, the deer carelessly nipping away the candle of a pine.

And there is mischance as well. The woodsman finds the deer in spring, standing tall on dead legs with head caught in a tree's crotch as it reached for browse. The hunter stands, too pleased to shoot, watching the soaring rocket burst of partridges swooping away among the trees, but I have seen a bird impaled upon a sharp dead branch it did not see in time to swerve. A starling hangs itself between two wires. A skunk thrusts his head into a can, and starves. A frog sits disconsolately in a barrel in a spring, a place into which he hopped thankfully on a hot summer day, but from which he could not hop out again.

We think, quite naturally, of what we see. The free, vigorous, swinging, wild ones full of health and strength are what leap up before us in the fields. But mischance makes disaster in nature, as on parlor stairs, and we have common ground again to think on.

WINTER / PEACH LOG

Before the fire, when the quick brash flames from the kindling kick up over the back log and illuminate the dark and lovely grain, one is moved to meditate upon certain investment opportunities and their predictable returns: the miserly percentages over which rich men gloat, and the unending largess of the land. For the land gives its wealth unstintingly, even to those who put up only a sliver of their time and their desire as collateral. To the one who invests however modestly, but with care and affection, it returns not a fraction but a hundredfold, and forever. Forever, that is, as any one person is concerned with forever.

This log was peach: a pit, a decade and a half ago, among a thousand pits, of hybrids both controlled and free, from this and other climes. The planting entailed no more than the opening of a furrow and the turning of it again, and of waiting. No one can say what rare and delicate varieties of peach were here and never detected, for the squirrels took their harvest of some, and this was largess, if not to me then at least to my fellow investors. Afterward the rabbits took a share in the first and second year of the seedlings, and this too was a payment of dividends fully earned.

But from those twice-decimated ranks of treelets grew this tree and three others, which gave rise to a new variety of peaches. Not only mother of a flourishing line, it was itself borne down annually with a lush burden. Each year for five years it yielded three bushels of fruit, encapsuling the sweet savor of summer and releasing it in rich syrup when the world was white, a process which taught my children the beginning of economics and of treasuries having more to do with memories than money.

All this was my reward for an expenditure of a few hours a year, pruning, feeding, and occasionally fending off certain bugs and insects of aggressive intent. Then having lived its span and paid innumerable pluralities of cost for its place in the sun, the peach tree died. It stood a year more on the stump, wearing an unexpected but welcome garland of wild grapes in its drying branches. After that it came down, went to the saw and maul and wedges, and revealed the splendid corrugated grain that is as richly luminous as plum wine, and almost as dense as oak.

A friend mutters because the wood goes to the fire when it might be turned into a glossy lamp or worked into plaque or bowl. He does not understand my resistance and I cannot tell him, for I scarcely know myself. But before the fire, when the hot, hard wood begins to glow, a summation forms. Perhaps there is in each of us a right to complete our service and in ashes return to the earth again, and so balance the books.

81

WINTER / REDPOLL

The redpolls would have understood my father, who set out to journey into the south for the winter and settled close to the headwaters of the Namekagon. For the redpolls too have come south to winter here in what passes for a milder climate, relative to the utter arctic that is their true home, where even the dwarfed spruce gives way to the everlasting frost of tundra. They came with the snow, a bright scattering of finches that have not come in such numbers before. Having found my young birches, they'll come again, I hope.

They are as joyous as children on a holiday, which indeed they are: a movable convention of fifty birds, free and flirtatious as though there would never be another spring. If it is not exactly that they go where the action is, then they bring it with them. During nesting time, when they are at home in the far north, they scarcely sing, understandable in view of the locale, but here they are the most melodious of the native finches. They chirp and tweet and twitter like wild canaries, but with more song in them, more volume and variety.

With them now, as they swarm over the birches, are a couple of crossbills, their kissing cousins. It is a good thing to stay on friendly terms with such a cousin, if you are in a land of cone-bearing trees. The crossbills can break open a spruce cone easily, so that a redpoll can eat the seeds that spill, and since the crossbills do not appear to mind, it is a pleasant relationship. But it is the birches that redpolls like best of all, and the saucy little birds in the striped suits with the startling bright foreheads and the pink vests march up and down the branches, munching at seeds and winter buds and afterward gleaning the golden flakes of discard on the snow.

They are splendid guests. I open my door and walk out among them and they are unalarmed. If I have fresh seeds for the feeder they welcome me, and if I make no harsh movements or uncouth noises they shortly are all around me, commenting like chickadees, but in a busy and articulate swarm.

With luck, the redpolls will stay until spring, or what passes for spring in their understanding, for they will follow the retreating snow line home. But while they are here they will be cherished; we have too few such optimists among us at this season to let them go unnoticed or unrewarded.

WINTER / ORION

On sharp December nights, when the chickadee sleeps cozily beneath the shaggy bark of hickory and the owl's shadow leaves no track upon the snow, I have my reasons for walking my dogs. They may concern themselves with rabbits and with mice, if they will walk with me beyond the last house, past the yard lights that put a screen of trivial glare between me and the southern sky.

It is a moment to be stretched luxuriously: to walk a few yards farther than I must, and then to turn my head at last and see the constellation of Orion driving across that great black sweep of space.

When today's child looks upward, it is with a dream of passage. One child in two can still find the Big Dipper, and perhaps one in ten can run his eye from Merak through Dubhe and find Polaris, though he does not know their names. But only one in a hundred can point out Orion, not to mention the collateral certainty that when the Hunter is in the sky, then the wild meat is good for the taking.

There are other losses. One cannot learn to know Orion, the Hunter, in a single night, and the recurring periods of developing acquaintance become an inseparable part of life's experience.

I think perhaps the Hunter is best learned beside a campfire, when the frost is whitening on the tent where it lies in shadow, and from diverse men. First, the eye sees the mighty figure itself, knee lifted in stride, club upraised, dogs at his heel. Then, within the figure one sees the stars with names that have the rocking gait of camels: Alnitak, Alnilam, and Mintaka in the jeweled belt; Bellatrix, and the glowing ember of the dying Betelgeuse at the shoulders; and the icy brilliance of Rigel on the upward step, and Saiph behind.

On the left, the belt points out the hounds—the little dog Procyon, and Sirius, second only to our own sun for brightness and for nearness in our sky. A line from Rigel through Betelgeuse points to the twins, and Orion raises his left hand toward Aldebaran. From Orion, you can journey all around the winter sky and find names that recall great deeds and tragedies and triumphs, so that you will never thereafter be entirely alone at night, when you can see the stars.

My astronomical friends fret at all this. They want to lead me into the path of knowledge, of learning vast intricacies that I do not really need to know. They do not understand the extent of the resistance they labor against. I can summon up a time when there was a fire, and snow beyond the fire, and tired men and a small boy. As the firelight ebbed, the clouds thinned, and a very old man stood up at the edge of the fire and lifted a hand from the four-barred candy-striped blanket around his shoulders. At the edge of the fire he pointed south, saying urgently and fiercely, "Voila. Il grand chasseur. Him *mighty* hunter."

I think I never heard Orion spoken of so well again: Nor, to put myself obstinately against the tide of progress, do I wish it, even though I might stand to a point of a personal privilege. Orion stood due south at midnight on the night that I was born.

WINTER / CONCLUSION

Now we have come to the dead of winter, when the shining young god of light and peace lies slain; the warm blood congeals and frost crystals form within the hearts of those who love the light. It is not cold alone that drives the spirits down to match the mercury at the bottom of the glass; it is the darkness. Even man, the one animal who can control his own environment, can, if he tunes a sharp ear, hear the ancestral whisper in the hollow of his bones warning that the long northern nights and dim gray noons are heavy with disaster for those who must hunt by day.

There is good reason for the diurnal creature to fear the cold night: There may not be time enough to feed enough so that another frigid night can be endured. And the fires of life within a bird, like the furnace within a house, burn fuel in great gulps to keep back the encompassing cold.

A field biologist with a light meter can say when the partridge will leave the alder buds and abruptly turn to roost, and when the owl will stretch his wings, and when fold them. And, yes, a light meter can predict when the great geese suddenly raise their heads, yearning for the south, and when pheasant hens begin all at once in March to think of lime siftings along the roads, and the great task of egg laying, and when mysterious juices stir inexplicably within the bowels of animals whose grimmest struggle against starvation is yet to come.

If it were not for the winter solstice, perhaps we all would perish, with our hopes abandoned. But the great promise of the sun god's coming back has been made before, and kept. The legends of our mingled cultures share this story of resurrection: Wicked Loki has been banished, the mistletoe repents, and Baldur lives. In a few weeks the sap will rise in the maples although the earth remains like stone, and my impatient sparrow will scratch away the snow to reach the mulching hay and start another nest in the martin house. A season of birds will have come full circle, and life will begin again.